Negotiation Skills

90 Minute Guides

Michelle N. Halsey

Contents

Chapter 1 – Understanding Negotiation 5

Types of Negotiations 6

The Three Phases 7

Skills for Successful Negotiating 7

Chapter 2 – Getting Prepared 9

Establishing Your WATNA and BATNA 9

Identifying Your WAP 10

Identifying Your ZOPA 11

Personal Preparation 11

Chapter 3 – Laying the Groundwork 13

Setting the Time and Place 13

Establishing Common Ground 14

Creating a Negotiation Framework 15

The Negotiation Process 15

Chapter 4 – Phase One – Exchanging Information 19

Getting Off on the Right Foot 19

What to Share 20

What to Keep to Yourself 20

Chapter 5 – Phase Two – Bargaining 23

What to Expect 23

Techniques to Try 24

Ten Negotiation Techniques: 24

How to Break an Impasse 25

Chapter 6 – About Mutual Gain 27

Three Ways to See Your Options 27

About Mutual Gain 27

Creating a Mutual Gain Solution 28

What Do I Want? 29

What Do They Want?..30

What Do We Want? 30

Chapter 7 – Phase Three – Closing.......................................33

Reaching Consensus...33

Building an Agreement 34

Setting the Terms of the Agreement 34

Chapter 8 – Dealing with Difficult Issues............................37

Being Prepared for Environmental Tactics 37

Dealing with Personal Attacks 38

Controlling Your Emotions..39

Deciding When It's Time to Walk Away 39

Chapter 9 – Negotiating Outside the Boardroom..................41

Adapting the Process for Smaller Negotiations 41

Negotiating via Telephone 41

Negotiating via Email 42

Chapter 10 – Negotiating on Behalf of Someone Else 45

Choosing the Negotiating Team...45

Covering All the Bases...46

Dealing with Tough Questions...46

Additional Titles...49

Chapter 1 – Understanding Negotiation

Although people often think of boardrooms, suits, and million dollar deals when they hear the word "negotiation," the truth is that we negotiate all the time. For example, have you ever:

- Decided where to eat with a group of friends?

- Decided on chore assignments with your family?

- Asked your boss for a raise?

These are all situations that involve negotiating! This workshop will give participants an understanding of the phases of negotiation, tools to use during a negotiation, and ways to build win-win solutions for all those involved.

By the end of this tutorial, you will be able to:

- Understand the basic types of negotiations, the phases of negotiations, and the skills needed for successful negotiating

- Understand and apply basic negotiating concepts: WATNA, BATNA, WAP, and ZOPA

- Lay the groundwork for negotiation

- Identify what information to share and what to keep to yourself

- Understand basic bargaining techniques

- Apply strategies for identifying mutual gain

- Understand how to reach consensus and set the terms of agreement

- Deal with personal attacks and other difficult issues

- Use the negotiating process to solve everyday problems

- Negotiate on behalf of someone else

Understanding Negotiation

Before we get started, let's take a look at two basic types of negotiation. We'll consider the three phases of negotiation and the skills you need to become an effective negotiator.

Types of Negotiations

The two basic types of negotiations require different approaches.

Integrative negotiations are based on cooperation. Both parties believe they can walk away with something they want without giving up something important. The dominant approach in integrative negotiations is problem solving. Integrative negotiations involve:

- Multiple issues. This allows each party to make concessions on less important issues in return for concessions from the other party on more important issues.

- Information sharing. This is an essential part of problem solving.

- Bridge building. The success of integrative negotiations depends on a spirit of trust and cooperation.

Distributive negotiations involve a fixed pie. There is only so much to go around and each party wants as big a slice as possible. An example of a distributive negotiation is haggling over the price of a car with a car salesman. In this type of negotiation, the parties are less interested in forming a relationship or creating a positive impression. Distributive relationships involve:

- Keeping information confidential. For example, you don't want a car salesman to know how badly you need a new car or how much you are willing to pay.

- Trying to extract information from the other party. In a negotiation, knowledge truly is power. The more you know about the other party's situation, the stronger your bargaining position is.

- Letting the other party make the first offer. It might be just what you were planning to offer yourself!

The Three Phases

The three phases of a negotiation are:

1. Exchanging Information

2. Bargaining

3. Closing

These phases describe the negotiation process itself. Before the process begins, both parties need to prepare for the negotiation. This involves establishing their bargaining position by defining their BATNA, WATNA, and WAP (see Module Three). It also involves gathering information about the issues to be addressed in the negotiation.

After the negotiation, both parties should work to restore relationships that may have been frayed by the negotiation process.

It is essential to pay attention to all the phases of negotiation. Without the first phase, the exchange of information, and the establishment of bargaining positions, the second phase cannot happen in any meaningful sense because no one knows where they stand. It sets a scene for demands to be manageable and reasonable. Negotiations are, after all, about the art of the possible. Without the third phase, anything that has been decided during phase two cannot be formalized and will not take hold – leading to the necessity for further negotiation or an absolute breakdown in a relationship.

Skills for Successful Negotiating

Key skills include:

- Effective speaking

- Effective listening

- A sense of humor

- A positive attitude

- Respect

Without the above factors, negotiations will be difficult if not impossible. The necessity for negotiation arises because neither party will be able to get everything they want. Knowing that there must be concessions, each party in the negotiation is required to adopt an attitude of understanding that they must get the best deal possible in a way which is acceptable to the other party. The importance of effective speaking and listening is clear; it is necessary to establish what you are looking for and what you are prepared to accept, while understanding what the other parties will be happy with.

A sense of humor and a positive attitude are essential because they allow for a sense of give and take. Negotiations can become fraught, and having the ability to see the other side's point of view while being sanguine with regard to what you can achieve will be essential. Of course you will want as much as you can get – but the other side needs to achieve what they can, too. Seriously uneven negotiations will simply lead to further problems along the line. An atmosphere of respect is essential. If you do not make concessions while demanding them from your counterpart, it makes for a negotiation which will end in dissatisfaction.

However important a sense of understanding for your "opponent" may be, it is also necessary to have the confidence to not settle for less than you feel is fair. Good negotiators understand the importance of balance. Yes, you will have to make concessions, but the point of making concessions is to secure what you can get – so you need to pay attention to your bottom line and ensure you are not beaten down to a minimum. Knowing what is realistic, and ensuring that you can get the best deal, relies on being ready to insist upon something that the other side may not be willing to give initially. Emotional intelligence, persistence, patience, and creativity can all play a part here.

Chapter 2 – Getting Prepared

Like any challenging task, negotiation requires preparation. Before you begin a negotiation, you need to define what you hope to get out of it, what you will settle for, and what you consider unacceptable. You also need to prepare yourself personally. The key to personal preparation is to approach the negotiation with self-confidence and a positive attitude.

Without this preparation, you will end up giving more than you get from negotiations. It may be unavoidable that you will have to give up more than you would ordinarily be willing to, but finding the balance between acceptable concessions and getting the best deal for yourself relies on you being ready to go into negotiations with the strongest bargaining position you can.

Establishing Your WATNA and BATNA

In most negotiations, the parties are influenced by their assumptions about what they think are the alternatives to a negotiated agreement. Often the parties have an unrealistic idea of what these alternatives are, and they are unwilling to make concessions because they think they can do just as well without negotiating. If you do not have a clear idea of your **WATNA (Worst Alternative to a Negotiated Agreement) and BATNA (Best Alternative to a Negotiated Agreement)**, you will negotiate poorly based on false notions about what you can expect without an agreement.

Often the parties in a negotiation need to decide how likely a particular outcome will be. If your WATNA is something that would be difficult for you to accept, but the likelihood of it happening is small, you might not feel compelled to give up much in negotiations. Realism is essential in this situation. If you could have the ideal situation, the "blue sky" scenario, negotiations would not be necessary. In order to focus on the negotiations with a sense of purpose, your WATNA is important. What is often referred to as the "worst case scenario" is something that any sensible person will think about before embarking on any initiative. What if it goes wrong? How will we deal with that? How you feel about the WATNA will dictate how flexible you need to be (and therefore will be) in negotiations.

The BATNA is almost more important than the WATNA. If you look at your situation in the absence of a negotiated agreement, and find it almost unthinkable, you will be pressed to enter negotiations in the hope of getting a satisfactory agreement. The word "satisfactory" is important here. Is the WATNA better than satisfactory? Is the BATNA worse? Generally, people only enter into negotiations because they feel they have to. They arrive at this conclusion based on analysis of their WATNA and BATNA.

Identifying Your WAP

In any negotiation, it is important that you keep your **WAP (Walk Away Price)** to yourself, especially if it is significantly less than your initial offer. If the other party knows that you will be willing to take a lot less than you are offering, then you will be negotiating from a position of weakness. If the other party knows, or has an idea of your WAP then it stops being your WAP and simply becomes your price. Establishing a WAP in your mind, and ensuring that those negotiators on your side of the bargain (and only they) know it, allows you to take your strongest possible bargaining position. The other party will try to argue you down from your proposed price, so you will need to remain firm. If they want to pay less, then you may be prepared to agree on a lower price in return for concessions.

The opposing party will then have to consider what is acceptable to them. Rather than push too hard and lose out on a deal which would be beneficial to themselves, they will have their own areas where they are willing to make concessions. However, if they know that you have set a WAP that would save them money, they will simply hold firm at that price. They have no incentive to make concessions to you. In many ways, negotiation is about keeping as much to yourself as you possibly can until you can no longer maintain that position.

Once you have set your WAP, it is essential to keep to it. A walk away price becomes absolutely meaningless if you are not prepared to walk away should it not be met. You should give the impression to opponents in negotiation that you could walk away at any time. They will, after all, not be prepared to stop once they get a price which is satisfactory to them – they will look to wring a bit more value out of the deal for themselves, testing you to see what you will give up. A warning against setting your WAP unrealistically low is that the other party will not take you seriously if you are a pushover in negotiations. They will seek to test you at every turn.

Identifying Your ZOPA

In the negotiation for the used car, both parties should feel good about the outcome. Even though the parties might have hoped for a better deal, both got a better price than their WAP.

This negotiation demonstrates the importance of keeping your WAP to yourself if you want to negotiate the best deal. Your range in this situation falls between the price that you would ideally, realistically get and the WAP you have set. In an ideal world you could demand a million dollars and expect to get it. In a realistic world, you need to be realistic in negotiations.

You should arrive at your ideal realistic price by seeing what the accepted market value for what you are offering is. By adjusting for your specific negotiating position (whether you are approaching it from a position of need, etc.), you can find your best realistic price. Then think about a price at which it would no longer be worthwhile to strike a deal.

Your co-negotiator will have done the same. What he hopes to pay and what you hope to get are just that – hopeful. The **ZOPA (Zone Of Possible Agreement)** is the area in which the final price will sit, and within that ZOPA you will ideally end up with a price closer to their WAP than yours. If you hint at where your WAP is, the other party will be less likely to come to an agreement that is substantially better than that.

Personal Preparation

One way to relieve some of the tension you may be feeling before a negotiation is to remind yourself that there is nothing to be afraid of. As long as you understand your position, there is no danger that you will "lose" the negotiation. During and before negotiation you should always be:

- Polite - It never reduces your argument

- Firm - Removes Perceptions of Weakness

- Calm - Facilitates Persuasion and Compromise

- Do not take things personally

Knowing your position before entering negotiations means that you are sure of your "red lines". Things that you are not prepared to consider that would make your position worse than it is now. Many people get pushed into a deal which is unsatisfactory to them because they have failed to prepare for the negotiation in this way. If you go into negotiations with vague ideas, that vagueness will become a weakness in your negotiating position.

The important thing about your position in negotiations is that you should be the only one who knows what it is. Many people compare negotiation to a game of poker. When playing poker you should always be careful to keep to yourself what kind of hand you have. If your opponent knows your position, they will squeeze you to its very limits, confident that you have no strong impetus to push back.

When a negotiator knows that their "opponent" has a weak or compromised position, they will instinctively know that they are negotiating with someone who is working from a position of desperation. They will believe "that's what he's decided he is willing to settle for, because he needs this deal. Does he need it enough to give me a little bit more leverage?", and will negotiate from that standpoint.

Chapter 3 – Laying the Groundwork

In the previous module, we looked at the importance of establishing your bargaining position. In this module we consider other aspects of preparation: setting the time and place, establishing common ground, and creating a negotiating framework. Even at this early stage it is important to have certain principles in place. If you allow them to be compromised, then you will already have put yourself in a position where you can be considered as prey for hostile negotiators. Getting the groundwork in place may seem like a formality, but it is the first stage of negotiations, and therefore as much a part of the arrangements as any other.

Setting the Time and Place

Setting the time and place can give you an advantage in a negotiation. People feel most comfortable conducting a negotiation on their home turf. Most people have a particular time of day when they feel most alert and clear-headed.

Environmental factors can interfere with negotiations, for example:

- A noisy setting

- Frequent interruptions

- Crowded conditions

- Lack of privacy

If you are conducting a negotiation at your own site, you have control over most of these things. If you are negotiating at the other party's site, ask the other party to remedy these conditions as much as possible before negotiations begin.

In sport, every game takes place at a venue, and in most cases one of the parties involved will be the "home team". In the vast majority of cases, where the parties are evenly matched in terms of talent and preparation, the team that wins will be the home team. They are playing in familiar surroundings, where things such as climate and ambient noise are to their advantage. The away team spends the early part of the game acclimatizing to their unfamiliar surroundings.

In political negotiations leading on from a war (or trying to prevent one), there is a tendency to hold the discussions in a neutral venue, where both parties are equally unfamiliar with the surroundings, meaning that neither has the advantage and allowing the negotiations to be even-handed. In business, it is rare to have the opportunity to hold negotiations in a neutral venue, and frequently there will be a "home side".

The time of negotiations is also important. Human beings are always in some part at the mercy of their "biorhythms" which cause the body and the mind to function differently at different times of day. Some people, as you will know, tend to be "morning people" while others are more comfortable the longer the day goes on. If you want to build in an advantage in negotiations, it is worth making sure either that the negotiations are held at your home venue, at your most comfortable time of day, or both. Sometimes there will be debate about the setting for a negotiation – and often, this is where the first negotiations and concessions will take place.

Establishing Common Ground

Sometimes the parties in a negotiation begin by discussing the issue on which they are farthest apart. It might seem like they are working hard, but they are not working effectively.

It is often more effective to begin by discussing what the parties agree on and then move to an issue on which they are close to agreement. Then they can take on progressively tougher issues until they reach the issue on which they are farthest apart. This gradual approach sets a positive tone for the negotiation. It also helps the two parties get into a pattern of thinking about issues in terms of shared interests.

Momentum is an important thing in negotiations. If the meeting is continually stalled by disputes over the smallest of issues, the outcome is likely to be less desirable for both parties as the goodwill which is necessary to drive negotiations forward will be extremely thin on the ground. For this reason, having an agenda which is stacked in favor of positive items at the beginning is a way that will work best for both sides. Concessions will have to happen in the end, but if both sides are in a positive frame of mind it creates a positive dynamic in which to negotiate.

Creating a Negotiation Framework

Both sides in a negotiation bring their own frame of reference based on their experience, values, and goals. For a negotiation to proceed, the two sides have to agree to a common framework. They need to agree on what issues are being addressed. Sometimes the way these issues are stated will influence the course of the negotiation. Each side would like to frame the issues in a way that furthers its goals. From this it is possible to see how involved negotiations can get. Sometimes people will use a phrase to describe preliminary negotiations: "talks about talks" – and this is a fairly interesting phrase, as it sheds light on just how much is up for debate in the average negotiation.

Before starting negotiations, it is essential to agree on which issues are up for negotiation and which are non-negotiable. Those issues which are non-negotiable are taken off the negotiating table and the parties endeavor to move forward with what they can negotiate on. It can also be decided what form of words will be used in the program for negotiations – making clear to both sides what matters are off limits, and why.

Without establishing a framework, negotiations can be extremely disorganized and lack direction. It helps to remember that trying to get a negotiated settlement between two parties who have their differences calls for a great deal of patience and acceptance on both sides that there will be some "medicine" to take – you don't want to take it, but it is necessary – and therefore it is important to make the pill as sweet as possible. Setting a positive framework for negotiations is all about sweetening the pill.

The Negotiation Process

| Preparation | Opening Position | Bargaining | Movement | Closing |

Preparation:

- Identify your key commitments

Opening Position:

- Outline Your Opening Position

- Decide whether this will be High Ball or Low Ball

- Ensure that this position is realistic in light of the facts available to both sides

- Allow for movement within whatever opening position you adopt

- Confirm all agreements reached and positions offered

Bargaining

- Question for Information

- Challenge other side for justifications of their position

- Examine and Test their commitment

- Present Your Key Commitments

- Explore Key Commitments

- Summarize Arguments and Seek Acceptance

- Look for Signals of Possible Movement

- Identify and Highlight Common Ground

Movement

- Be Prepared to Concede

- Begin with those of Low Priority and seek High Priority Items

- Never Concede on More than possible by your Brief

- Use your Concessions Wisely

- Don't just give these away expect and receive something in return

- Use Conditional Argument

- All Movement Should be realistic and contained within your brief

- It Should be always towards the other sides position and not away from it

- Be prepared for larger movements at first as it can build trust within the negotiation

- Continue with smaller movements

Closing

- Emphasize the benefits to both parties

- Carefully introduce the consequences of not reaching agreement to both parties and losing what has been agreed so far

- Timing is Essential

- Take Care when making a Final Offer. Be sure that it is consistent with your brief.

- A Small Traded Offer is often better. A small move by them in return for an extra movement by you.

- Ensure that all agreements are understood and accepted before finalization

- This should be well documented and signed at the close of the negotiations

- These should be then forwarded to both parties post negotiations

Chapter 4 – Phase One – Exchanging Information

The first phase in a negotiation involves an exchange of information. Both sides state their positions on the issues being addressed in a non-confrontational way. The tricky part of this phase is deciding what to reveal and what to hold back. The "poker" metaphor for negotiating is a very good one, because it describes exactly the way that negotiating parties will want to "allow" each other to think. The information you share with your negotiating counterpart will allow them to read a certain amount about your position. You cannot negotiate blindly, after all. However, too much information given away can really come back to bite you.

Getting Off on the Right Foot

Before you actually get down to work, it's a good idea to engage in a little small talk with the other participants in the negotiation. This will help set a positive tone. You might find that you have some things in common (such as hobbies or favorite teams) with the other participants.

If you rush right into the negotiation without some initial pleasantries, the other party may feel that you are being pushy and aggressive. For some people, this is a desirable negotiating style. However, it is advisable to have as many strings as possible to your bow when it comes to negotiations. Being "human" and easy to relate to is far less likely to persuade the other party that you are someone who needs to be kept in check, and may work to your advantage.

Obviously when it comes to introductions and preliminaries it is an idea not to get too informal. Apart from anything else, this will feel quite artificial when all parties are fully aware that there are issues to be debated here. Formality also lends itself to details being correct – how many negotiations, you have to wonder, have foundered at an early stage because one participant forgot the name of a counterpart or made an accidentally offensive remark due to ignorance of a critical detail?

Projecting an image of relaxed friendliness with an element of restraint is your best way to introduce yourself. By no means should you give the impression that you are here to bleed your counterpart dry – this will put them on the defensive and entrench their position, to your disadvantage – but it does help to project self-confidence. If you seem in a hurry to get negotiations completed and an agreement sealed, the impression will be that you want to escape from the whole process with a minimum of losses – which will not make you a formidable negotiating counterpart.

What to Share

At the start of a negotiation, you don't want to give a detailed statement about your position on specific issues. That is a subject for bargaining. If the other party tries to rush you into stating your bargaining position prematurely, say something like, "That's an important question. Before we get to that, let's make sure we agree on the issues we're discussing today."

It may be helpful to think why the other party would be in a hurry to get you to state your position. If they are fixated on that so early in negotiations, the chances are that they have been worrying about it for some time beforehand, and will want to get negotiations over and done with without having to worry about giving away more than they will need to. In such a case, it does you no harm at all to leave them waiting for this information by concentrating on laying down the framework.

In negotiations, one party's opinion on what should constitute the agenda will differ from the other at least in terms of how the issues should be framed. The same issue can be framed in several different ways, and a simple form of words can be quite contentious. Agreeing on the topics for discussion is something that allows both parties to find common ground, while preparing the way for both parties to recognize that they will not complete negotiations without making some movement on some issues.

What to Keep to Yourself

Holding back information can be a tricky business. You don't want to appear secretive or deceptive, but at the same time you don't want to give away your bargaining position prematurely. The best way to deal with this situation is to attempt to set the agenda for the negotiation. Say something like, "Let's get a few general issues settled before we get into specifics." At the start of negotiations both parties will, to some extent, be on the defensive and will want to get an impression of whom they are dealing with before they go any further.

By dealing with matters of agenda first, both parties get an opportunity to "size up" their counterpart and think about what they want to get from the negotiation and what they can get. The major benefit of these early discussions is that the first tentative negotiations can be made without making or breaking the whole process. From here it is possible to have a more realistic idea about who you are dealing with. This can influence how you carry on with the negotiations.

If you walk into negotiations and after preliminary introductions simply say "OK, so this is what we have come for, and we will walk away if we don't get it", then you might as well not be having a negotiation in the first place. Equally, if you hint early in negotiations that you are prepared to settle for a deal which more or less favors your counterpart, you are simply setting the scene for them to take everything you are prepared to offer and more besides. Your success in negotiations depends on knowing what to say, when to say it and when to be silent.

Chapter 5 – Phase Two – Bargaining

Now we have reached the heart of the negotiation process. This phase — bargaining — is what most people mean when they talk about negotiation. This module explains what to expect when you begin to bargain and what to do if you run into an impasse. It also describes some common bargaining techniques used by experienced negotiators.

What to Expect

In addition to learning about the pressures, targets, and needs that might influence your opponents, you might also want to try to get some idea of their usual negotiating approach.

- Do they typically start out with an unreasonable offer?

- Do they try to rush the negotiation?

- Do they try to frame the issues to their own advantage?

Finding this out can be a process of trial and error, but if you have any contacts in the same business who have negotiated with your opponent you can ask them for a rundown of how the negotiation went. This is something which will be familiar to any sports fan, in that teams and players will "scout" their opponents to exploit any weaknesses and prepare to deal with any strength that might make their opponent formidable.

If an opponent has a reputation for always looking to rush the negotiation, it is possible to use that to your advantage. By remaining firm on your bargaining position you will be able to place pressure on them to get the deal done on your terms. If they want it to be over quickly, they will be less likely to spend time wringing concessions out of you and will have to either spend longer in negotiations than they would ordinarily wish (potentially making them uncomfortable and prone to rash decisions) or make a concession in order to get the arrangement in place quickly.

Finding out – and analyzing – your opponent's pressure, targets and needs is something that should be done if possible prior to your negotiations with them. If they give information in the preliminary stages of a meeting that may be of use to you, then by all means you can duly note that information and bring it into play later in negotiations at a key point. The more information you can find out in advance, the better for you. It will all be useful in negotiation settings.

Techniques to Try

Some of these techniques are what you might expect to encounter when dealing with a street vendor, but that doesn't keep more sophisticated business people from using them. The important thing is to recognize them and be prepared to respond to them if they are used against you in a negotiation. As long as you recognize the technique when it is used, you can actually turn them to your advantage in a pressurized negotiation setting.

One thing that many of the techniques have in common is that they tend to be used more in hope than in expectation. **The Exaggerated First Offer** technique is typically made in the full awareness that that offer will not be met, and the hope that somewhere between the $1000 you will settle for and the $2000 you have asked for, the dealer will make an offer which is as high as you can hope for. Experienced negotiators recognize this technique, and will usually respond with what may be an equally exaggerated counter-offer which undercuts what the car is worth.

The techniques tend not to have a lot to do with realism, essentially trying to create a circumstance whereby a customer feels rushed, belittled, or harried in some way into accepting a situation which is beneficial to the person using the technique. If a customer feels that it is a choice between paying $1,500 today or $3,000 next week, they will usually plump for the former – regardless of how true the pitch was in the first place. As well as this, some negotiators will attempt to flatter you by saying "OK, normally I wouldn't go anywhere near this low, but because I like you, here is what I'm going to do". If you have a firm line to hold to, keep holding it in the face of these techniques and you will hold the power.

Ten Negotiation Techniques:

1. Prepare, prepare, prepare.

2. Pay attention to timing.

3. Leave behind your ego.

4. Ramp up your listening skills.

5. If you don't ask, you don't get.

6. Anticipate compromise.

7. Offer and expect commitment.

8. Don't absorb their problems.

9. Stick to your principles.

10. Close with confirmation.

How to Break an Impasse

The dictionary says an impasse is a noun which describes: "a situation in which no progress is possible, especially because of disagreement; a deadlock".

There are a number of ways to break an impasse in negotiations. Here are a few:

- If the impasse involves money, change the terms: a larger deposit, a shorter pay period, etc.

- Change a team member or the team leader.

- Agree on easy issues and save the more difficult issues for later.

- Change the list of options being considered.

- Agree to adjourn for a fixed period of time to try to come up with other options.

The risk with an impasse in negotiations is that it can become a point where any movement from either party will be seen as weakness. The impasse can become the overall focus of the spell of negotiations, where the actual focus should be that which is set out in the initial framework as agreed in the preliminary stages. Sometimes in politics, negotiations take years to reach their fruition, because sticking points are occasionally unavoidable. In business, it tends not to take that long – but it is essential that you deal with impasses as they occur.

If you want to get around an impasse, the realization needs to be made that it is happening for a reason and that overcoming it will necessitate changing something about the way you are negotiating. If you can see the sticking point, then by all means make that the focus of your change, but failing that it can be a good idea to place to problem on the back burner and deal with something else – something manageable which will enable the momentum to be put back in your negotiations.

Chapter 6 – About Mutual Gain

In their classic book *Getting to Yes*, Roger Fisher and William Ury argue that most negotiations are not as efficient or as successful as they might be because people tend to argue about positions rather than interests. Once the parties in a negotiation commit themselves to a position, they feel that changing their position represents failure. Instead, Fisher and Ury suggest that the parties in a negotiation focus on their interests. What can we get out of the negotiation that will further our interests? That is the question that should guide a negotiation toward achieving mutual gain.

Three Ways to See Your Options

Positional Bargaining: Soft	Positional Bargaining: Hard	Interest Bargaining
Participants want to be friends.	Participants are adversaries.	Participants are problem solvers.
The gal is agreement.	The goal is victory.	The goal is an outcome that will satisfy the interests of the participants.
Participants trust each other.	Participants distrust each other.	Participants treat trust and distrust as irrelevant.
Participants are soft on the people and the problem.	Participants are hard on the people and the problem.	Participants are soft on the people, hard on the problem.
Participants change positions readily	Participants stick to a position	Participants focus on interests, not positions
Participants state their bottom line	Participants conceal their bottom line	Participants don't have a bottom line
Participants make concessions	Participants demand concessions	Participants invent options for mutual gain
Participants search for one solution	Participants demand one solution	Participants develop multiple options

About Mutual Gain

The key to making the mutual gain approach work is to focus on interests, not positions. Both parties want to create an atmosphere of respect and order in the schools. What options are available to allow them to satisfy their interests?

The answer in this situation may be a compromise. One party wants uniforms, the other does not. The reasons why the first party wants to have uniforms is to avoid a situation where every student wears their own clothes and – potentially – bullying can arise where one person or group act with hostility towards another who have their own individual style. Although individuality is to be encouraged, it has its drawbacks when it leads to marked difference.

One potential answer is to not have a specific uniform requirement – where everyone wears the same clothes – as this has its own drawbacks, making students easily identifiable to outsiders and potentially causing problems for parents with limited financial means. Instead, a dress code can be implemented which requires students to dress in a certain way without necessarily dressing all the same. The dress code can stipulate that the students dress in a modest, reasonable way without necessarily being clones of one another. This allows both parties to get something of what they want, without either side having to give up too much.

Creating a Mutual Gain Solution

Creating a mutual gain solution requires some activities not usually associated with negotiations, for example:

- Brainstorming to "expand the pie" by coming up with a range of options

- Identifying shared values to help create options that will meet the interests of both parties

- Changing the scope of the negotiation — making it larger or smaller

- Identifying issues that can be set aside for future negotiations

One of the problems that arise in negotiations is that parties can feel that they are being marginalized in terms of what they can do and what they can get. They may feel that being in constant opposition means that the negotiations advance at a snail's pace if at all. In order to put in place a mindset where there is a chance for consensus, the parties can look at what unites them rather than what puts them in opposition to one another.

The difficulty in any negotiation arises when there are issues where both parties have a philosophical WAP which is too far from that of the other. There is in this case no ZOPA, and no matter how much negotiation takes place there will be a sticking point. If you can remove the sticking point from the equation at least temporarily, you can get in place a situation where there is space for consensus.

The danger of "ignoring the elephant in the room" is that it will not go away just because it is ignored. It will still be there, and although it is tempting to look at things from a "blue sky" point of view and forget about the clouds forming overhead, you can end up saving up problems for the latter stages of negotiations. What you could look at doing is having someone working away from the negotiating table to find a compromise solution, and bring it back to the table when it looks more palatable to both parties.

What Do I Want?

To begin, identify what you personally want out of the negotiation. Try to state this positively.

Examples:

- I want a fair share of all new customers.

- I want a better working relationship with my manager.

- I want changes to the schedule.

You can create two versions of your personal needs statement: your ideal resolution and your realistic resolution. Or, you could frame your statement into several steps if the negotiation is complicated.

Another useful exercise is to break down your statement into wants and needs. This is particularly valuable if your statement is vague. Let's take the statement, "I want changes to the schedule," as an example.

Want	Need
More input into the scheduling process	To work less than 30 hours per week
A more regular schedule	More notice for schedule changes

This will give you some bargaining room during the negotiation process, and will help ensure that you get what you need out of the solution. In the example above, you may be willing to give up a more regular schedule if more notice for schedule changes is provided.

What Do They Want?

Next, identify what the person that you are in conflict with wants. Try to frame this positively. Explore all the angles to maximize your possibilities for mutual gain.

These framing questions will help you start the process.

- What does my opponent need?

- What does my opponent want?

- What is most important to them?

- What is least important to them?

What Do We Want?

Now that you have identified the wants and needs of both sides, look for areas of overlap. These will be the starting points for establishing mutual ground.

Here is an example. Joe and George are in conflict over the current schedule. As the most senior members of the assembly line team, they both alternate their regular duties with that of foreman. Although taking on the responsibility gives the foreman an extra $250 per shift, the foreman also has to work an extra hour per shift, and has additional safety responsibilities.

Joe and George both work Monday to Friday. As a regular assembly line team member, their shifts are from 8:30 a.m. to 4:30 p.m. As foreman, they are expected to work from 8 a.m. to 5 p.m.

	Joe	George
Wants	• To have at least two foreman shifts per week.	• To have at least two foreman shifts per week. • To leave by 4:30 p.m. on Fridays.
Needs	• To leave by 4:30 p.m. on Mondays and Wednesdays to pick up his children. • To ensure that the foreman position is covered by someone from Monday to Friday, 8 a.m. to 5 p.m.	• Not to have more than three foreman shifts per week as it will require him to pay extra taxes. • To ensure that the foreman position is covered by someone from Monday to Friday, 8 a.m. to 5 p.m.

From this simple chart, we can see that Joe and George have the same goal: to ensure that the foreman position is covered by someone during regular working hours. Thus, this is a logistical conflict rather than an emotional one. We can also see from the chart that there seems to be some good starting ground for a solution.

When working through the wants and needs of both parties, be careful not to jump to conclusions. Rather, be on the lookout for the root cause. Often, the problem is not what it seems.

Chapter 7 – Phase Three – Closing

The final phase of a negotiation is a time for reaching consensus and building an agreement. A little hard work in this phase can ensure that the negotiation achieves it desired results.

Closing a negotiation can mean two different things: First it may be a question of how to bring different ideas to a mutually agreed conclusion. A second possibility view of 'closing' is what means negotiating parties can use to acknowledge or formalize the idea that agreement has been reached.

Recognizing that parties have reached agreement can be quite simple. One can ask the other(s), "Then, have we reached agreement?" The parties can shake hands, make a public announcement, or sign a document. The real issue is that each has to make it clear to other negotiators that a mutually agreed conclusion has indeed been reached.

Reaching Consensus

People have different ideas about what constitutes consensus. When applied to negotiations, consensus usually involves substantive agreement on key issues. Not everyone needs to be completely satisfied to reach consensus, but everyone needs to feel that the outcome of the negotiation is something they can live with. Building consensus is one of the hardest parts of negotiation, because the negotiating parties will potentially have radically different attitudes to what they feel the results should be.

Consensus has different meanings to different people. To some, it is unsatisfactory compromise, with both parties ending on a solution which does not give them everything they want. However, the simple fact is that you cannot please all of the people all of the time. Consensus is about pleasing as many people as far as possible. The best solutions, in reality, are the ones which leave nobody *too* displeased. In an ideal world you could please everyone equally and completely. But this world is not ideal, and the realities dictate that to please one person you will usually have to displease someone else.

This is why you have concessions: if you push for 100%, it is possible to end up with 0%. It is much better, therefore, to have two parties who each have a significant percentage of what they want. Reaching a consensus may have a bittersweet taste for some parties, but it is better to have 50% of something than 100% of nothing.

Building an Agreement

Building an agreement takes a special skill — the ability to translate generalities into specifics. Negotiators should realize that at this stage of the process the bargaining is over. They should try to create an agreement based on a fair and accurate interpretation of the consensus the parties have reached. At the same time they want to be careful they do not inadvertently give something up by not paying close enough attention to the written agreement.

Sometimes in negotiations, there can be a tendency to arrive at certain principle agreements and think that the job has been done. There is more to negotiation than offering a concession here and stipulating a limit there. If you make the mistake of thinking that the negotiation process has ironed out all of the problems in a deal, then you will find that there is a nasty shock waiting for you when you come to formalize the agreement.

It may help to think of the negotiation process as a news broadcast. It is great to have headlines that will make people sit up and take notice, but in order for these headlines to actually have any meaning it is necessary to write the stories. While the basic principle agreement reached in the negotiation room will be the headline, and what sticks in people's minds, it needs to be backed up with details. A good negotiations team will have at least one "details guy (or gal)" who is able to get the small print in place after the negotiators have put the outline in front of them.

Setting the Terms of the Agreement

We are all familiar with what can happen when the terms of an agreement are not clearly spelled out. For example:

Two employees agree on their individual responsibilities for updating their company's website. A week goes by and nothing has happened. Each person was waiting for the other one to take the first step. They had defined their responsibilities but they had not formulated a plan for carrying them out.

For an agreement to be successful, all the essential terms must be clearly stated in writing. It is quite one thing to have an agreement in theory but it will be essentially meaningless without the practicalities. The agreement which emerges at the end of negotiations needs to be backed up with the "how" factor. What emerges from the initial negotiation is what you are going to go, and possibly when. The "how" is the most important of all, though, as without the firm details of how you are going to put everything in place you can agree whatever you want and it will not matter.

Chapter 8 – Dealing with Difficult Issues

Most people are willing to negotiate in good faith. They don't resort to tricks or intimidation. Every once in a while, though, you might encounter someone who takes a less principled approach. You need to be prepared to deal with people who don't play fair. It is not cynicism to prepare for the possibility that someone will try to bend the rules, especially when those rules are unwritten. It is simply good preparation, and realism. Some people are unscrupulous, but if you know how to handle them it need not be the end of the world.

Being Prepared for Environmental Tactics

Using environmental tactics to gain an advantage in a negotiation doesn't happen that often, but negotiators need to be prepared for it. One rather obvious case is the executive who refuses to come out from behind his desk and forces the other side to sit in visitors' chairs. If this should happen, the best response might be, "I'm sorry, but I need some space to spread out my notes. Is there a conference room available?"

The host of the negotiations is in a position of power. To deny that this is the case would be wholly naïve and counter-productive. However, the way they use this power will differ between hosts. Sometimes you will come up against a host who turns conditions to their advantage, and if you do not at least say something about it you run the risk of your "opponent" feeling that they can do and say anything and get away with it. Even if you merely make a request for an improvement in the conditions, you will make them aware that you have noticed what they have done.

It may be that you feel you can deal with any environmental tactics that are thrown at you. If you show an ability to negotiate competently despite the conditions which have been foisted upon you, this may well win you the respect of your opponent. You should not have to do this, though, and it is sensible to put your opponent on notice that you will not be messed around – politely, but firmly if necessary.

Dealing with Personal Attacks

Any negotiation will be more productive if you are able to focus on problems and not personalities. Unfortunately, the other parties in the negotiation may not take this approach.

There are a number of reasons why negotiators sometimes engage in personal attacks:

- They may think that this type of behavior will give them an advantage in the negotiation.

- They may see any disagreement with their position as a threat to their self-image.

- They may feel that they are not being treated fairly or respectfully.

Sometimes you can avert personal attacks by demonstrating from the very start that you respect the other parties and their positions. A respectful opening sets a positive tone for the negotiation.

If the other party resists your efforts to establish an atmosphere of mutual respect, you might try saying something like, "Let's get back to the issues." If the other party still engages in personal attacks, it may be time to suspend the negotiation. Personal attacks are never helpful, although there may be some people on the opposite side who feel that by acting or speaking in an abusive manner they can intimidate you.

The advice given by many a parent to the child who has been the subject of teasing in the schoolyard does apply here. What someone says something against you; it often says more about them than it does about you. It is wise to take account of the factors which have led to their behavior – it may have come at a particularly emotional point in negotiations, or they may just have been attempting to assert some kind of superiority over you. By maintaining your dignity, you will be held in high regard.

It helps no-one if you respond in kind to personal attacks. All that will do is give the person who attacked you the reaction which tells them that they have scored a direct hit. You will do better by simply requesting to get on with negotiations and ignore unhelpful contributions. It may seem like an attempt to back out of a confrontation, but it is no sign of weakness if you refuse to respond to childishness.

Controlling Your Emotions

Recognizing and controlling emotions is an aspect of "emotional intelligence."

Emotional intelligence is different from what might be called academic intelligence, the type of intelligence that enables some people to get good grades in school and score well on standardized tests. More and more people are realizing that it takes more than just this type of intelligence to succeed in the workplace and in life.

In a negotiation, emotional intelligence involves recognizing how you and the other party are responding emotionally to the discussion. If the emotional temperature in the room seems to be heating up, you may decide that it's time to take a break. There is little benefit to allowing a negative atmosphere to build in a boardroom and turn into something which can torpedo negotiations at a delicate stage.

You will recognize when the emotional temperature is rising beyond where it should be, because discussions will become less focused, voices will be raised and the silences will be all the more silent. At this point in negotiations it might be wise to suggest a short break for everyone to go and have a coffee, or take some fresh air. You can then come back to the negotiations with the atmosphere cleared somewhat and try to make some progress without the risk of people losing their temper.

Deciding When It's Time to Walk Away

It would be wonderful if the atmosphere of every negotiation was warm and friendly, but that's not the way things work in the real world. By their very nature, negotiations involve a kind of adversarial relationship. For a negotiation to proceed, the two parties do not need to have friendly relations, but they do need to keep personal conflicts and unfair tactics from interfering with the process.

It's time to walk away from a negotiation if:

- The other party makes you feel threatened or extremely uncomfortable.

- The other party uses unfair tactics that make it impossible to have an equitable negotiation.

You may feel like walking away is an admission of defeat, and this may inspire you to try and make things work even when the prospect of that happening is becoming more and more remote. However, there are times when the other party simply crosses a line, and you would be well advised to show them that this is not going to be permitted. Calling an end to the meeting, with an invitation to recommence negotiations at a later date, may be the best thing for everyone.

Some negotiators use tactics which are simply and purely threatening to try and ensure that you bend to their will. The reason that many people do this is because it often works. It will, however, only work if it is allowed to work. If people walked away from negotiations every time someone tried to cheat them or intimidate them, then that kind of tactic would die out. It is good to have principles in this regard, because no-one ever got a good deal by making concessions to a threatening negotiator.

Chapter 9 – Negotiating Outside the Boardroom

Negotiating isn't just something that takes place in conference rooms with powerful forces aligned on either side of a table. People have informal negotiations every day — with their coworkers, merchants, even family members.

Adapting the Process for Smaller Negotiations

Some of the principles of negotiation can be useful in everyday situations. For example:

- Separate the people from the problem. Don't let personalities get in the way of negotiating.

- Focus on interests, not positions. Consider what both parties want and need. Don't let adherence to a particular position narrow the range of options you are willing to consider.

- Expand the range of options. One way to overcome an impasse in a negotiation is to expand the range of the discussion.

- State the terms of an agreement in specific, clear terms.

Even if you are not in a traditional negotiation position, it can be helpful to use the principles of negotiation to bring you a positive outcome in everyday life. Making decisions in the home, you will find that results can be found which are to the benefit of all parties by using these principles. It should be added that you would be ill advised to use these principles for every decision – but where there is some difficulty in reaching a decision, you can reach a positive outcome by taking into account some sound, decent principles which have for years been used to reach positive decisions.

Negotiating via Telephone

The phone can be a convenient vehicle for negotiations, especially when the two parties find it difficult to meet in person. But in many cases an agreement reached over the phone needs to be confirmed through some other method.

For example, suppose you have a phone conversation with a coworker in which you both agree to do certain things within the next week. A week goes by and the other person has not done what he agreed to. You call him and he replies, "I didn't agree to that." It would have been better to follow up the first phone call with an email message that begins, "I just want to confirm what we agreed to do in our phone conversation."

When you arrive at a positive conclusion from a phone negotiation, it can be tempting to just hold on to your belief that you have got the right result, but even if you have recorded the call an unscrupulous counterpart can try to back out of it if they feel they have plausible deniability. Get everything nailed down by following up, and you will be able to put the deal in the record books. It is common sense to keep everything regulated and avoid any difficulties further down the line.

In order to negotiate effectively on the telephone we need to consider a few rules that also apply to face-to-face negotiation:

- Pay attention to particular points.

- Listen Actively. Don't interrupt the other party; don't spend your 'listening time' figuring out how you're going to respond to them when they finally stop talking. The better you listen, the better you can learn, and the more likely you will be able to respond in a way that improves the negotiation's result.

- Don't let the immediacy of a telephone call force you into fast, unwise decisions. There is nothing wrong with requesting more time to think about the terms discussed.

Negotiating via Email

Email can be an effective method of communication, but is has some inherent limitations.

In general, it is appropriate to use email in a negotiation:

- When the topic is clearly defined.

- When the topic does not require extensive discussion

- When the expected response is relatively simple

- When there is little possibility of misunderstanding

It is not appropriate to use email:

- When the topic is complex

- When the topic requires extensive discussion

- When the topic has great personal significance for the parties involved

- When the topic is likely to stir up strong emotions

E-mail has become a very popular way of keeping discussions simple and straightforward both in business and personal communications. However, there are limitations to it and it is important to be aware of these limitations. Keeping communications simple and somewhat informal can be helpful, but it should be remembered that waiting on an e-mail can be frustrating. If multiple communications are required, it is best to keep things face-to-face.

What e-mail does have going for it in a negotiation framework is that it keeps a record of every e-mail sent and received, along with dates and times allowing everything to be official. If you have a relatively simple detail or two to be finalized, e-mail is fine. If you have a situation requiring a full negotiation, e-mail should only be used as a preparation aid and a formal confirmation of things decided in a full, face-to-face negotiation.

Chapter 10 – Negotiating on Behalf of Someone Else

Negotiating on behalf of someone else presents some special challenges. When you begin such a negotiation, you need to have a clear idea of your Walk Away Price (WAP) and the concessions you have permission to make. You also need to be sure you understand the issues well enough to respond to tough questions that may come up in the negotiation.

If you are assembling a team to assist in the negotiation, you need to select people who have the expertise and the temperament to move the negotiation forward. It is not unlike selecting an army unit, in some ways. When going into battle, you want to have people nearby who will ensure that your interests are protected. It is said that a chain is only as strong as its weakest link, and this is a good principle to take with you into negotiations.

Choosing the Negotiating Team

An essential part of leading a team of any kind is sharing information. Teams need information to thrive. Before the negotiation, hold a meeting with the team to make sure everyone has the information they need to make an effective contribution. You can also use these meetings to:

- Remind everyone of the team's goals

- Ensure that everyone understands his or her role in the negotiation

- Create a "game plan" for the negotiation

You do not want to approach negotiations with a team containing someone who is unaware of their role or of the overall goal. If there is uncertainty in the team, it will spread quickly and it will certainly be picked up on by your counterparts. This can lead to you being hamstrung in terms of your bargaining power, because a team with a clearly defined brief and all its members fully apprised of the plan will be able to pull concessions from one with chaos in its ranks.

Having a team with clearly defined roles and a clearly defined goal is something that will be an asset in any negotiations. The more people you have (as long as they are professional and aware of their position), the more talents at your disposal and the more room for maneuver you will have when it comes to intensive negotiations. What you want is a situation where "two heads are better than one", rather than one where "too many chefs spoil the broth".

Covering All the Bases

Some negotiations are so complex that it is difficult for one person to master all the issues. In these situations it is worthwhile to assemble a team of experts to make sure all the bases are covered. As with any team, it is important that each person knows exactly what he or she is responsible for. What is gained through having a dedicated team designed to achieve the best negotiating muscle can be lost through having people who are unaware of their roles or unclear on what they can and cannot deliver.

It is beneficial to have a team who feel that they can make decisions with an element of autonomy. This will allow them to operate naturally in a negotiation with little fear that they might overstep the mark. However, it is important to have some limitations to their autonomy, as they are not negotiating for themselves. There is a need for balance in these situations. If they feel their hands are tied and they cannot make a decision without referring back to you, they will be powerless in negotiations. If they feel that they have free rein and can do whatever they want, they may make a decision which you would not have made yourself and which damages your position. Finding the point in between where you can be confident that their decisions will benefit you is essential.

As with so many issues, it is important to get the balance right, as complex negotiations have a tendency to break down or end in an unpopular agreement if they are not handled correctly and with a sense of common purpose. If you get your team right, you can ensure at least that you are not the negotiator who ends up with an unpopular deal on your hands.

Dealing with Tough Questions

Here are some possible ways to respond to questions that you decline to answer:

- Suggest (in a friendly way) that the question is irrelevant. For example, you might say, "I'm not sure how that question fits in here."

- Say you don't know the answer. This is the best course of action to take if you really don't know the answer. This approach is better than guessing. As a next step, you might say that you will find out the answer and get back to the questioner within a day or two.

- Say that you would like to wait to respond to the question until later in the negotiation. This is the best thing to do if your answer will reveal too much about your position too soon.

- Reply with a question of your own. This may help clarify the motivation of the questioner. (What is the questioner really asking?)

Each of these approaches is a way that you can take the question in your stride and be seen to be giving it the consideration it deserves, without giving an answer that will put you on the back foot in terms of negotiations. People may ask you difficult questions in order to trap you, or because their own position is uncertain and they want to find a way to clarify it. How you handle such questions will be important, but as long as you show certainty and a desire to be straight with them, you need not lose confidence.

Additional Titles

The 90 Minute Guide series of books covers a variety of general business skills and are intended to be completed in 90 minutes or less. It is an effective way for building your skill set and can be used to acquire professional development units needed by project managers and other industries to maintain their certification. For the availability of titles please see https://www.silvercitypublications.com/shop/.

No. 1 - Appreciative Inquiry

No. 2 - Assertiveness and Self Control

No. 3 - Attention Management

No. 4 - Body Language Basics

No. 5 - Business Acumen

No. 6 - Business and Etiquette

No. 7 - Change Management

No. 8 - Coaching and Mentoring

No. 9 - Communications Strategies

No. 10 - Conflict Resolution

No. 11 - Creative Problem Solving

No. 12 - Delivering Constructive Criticism

No. 13 - Developing Creativity

No. 14 - Developing Emotional Intelligence

No. 15 - Developing Interpersonal Skills

No. 16 - Developing Social Intelligence

No. 17 - Employee Motivation

No. 18 - Facilitation Skills

No. 19 - Goal Setting and Getting Things Done

No. 20 - Knowledge Management Fundamentals

No. 21 - Leadership and Influence

No. 22 - Lean Process and Six Sigma Basics

No. 23 - Managing Anger

No. 24 - Meeting Management

No. 25 - Negotiation Skills

No. 26 - Networking Inside a Company

No. 27 - Networking Outside a Company

No. 28 - Office Politics for Managers

No. 29 - Organizational Skills

No. 30 - Performance Management

No. 31 - Presentation Skills

No. 32 - Public Speaking

No. 33 - Servant Leadership

No. 34 - Team Building for Management

No. 35 - Team Work and Team Building

No. 36 - Time Management

No. 37 - Top 10 Soft Skills You Need

No. 38 - Virtual Team Building and Management